LIVING CONSCIOUSLY IN GOD

THE AUTHOR

LIVING CONSCIOUSLY IN GOD

366 Themes for Daily Meditative Contemplation and Spiritual Enrichment

With Life-Enhancing Affirmations and Inspired Quotations

ROY EUGENE DAVIS

Center for Spiritual Awareness   Lakemont, Georgia

ISBN 978-0-87707-214-0

CSA Press, Publishers
Post Office Box 7
Lakemont, Georgia 30552
U.S.A.

The publishing department of
Center for Spiritual Awareness.
Offices and meditation retreat:
151 CSA Lane, Lakemont, Georgia
Off Lake Rabun Road.

PRINTED IN THE UNITED STATES OF AMERICA

Contents

Illustrations

PREFACE

An Invitation to Total Well-Being

Because only one ultimate Reality commonly referred to as God exists, and all souls are units of the pure essence of that Reality, we are always existing in it.

Until we are fully conscious of our true nature, it can be helpful to aspire to be spiritually enlightened, adhere to a holistic lifestyle, be higher purpose-directed, meditate superconsciously every day, and nourish the mind with constructive ideas.

Let the God-centered themes in the following pages daily motivate you to live skillfully and effectively while you gracefully grow to emotional and spiritual maturity.

Use the affirmations to arouse and bring forth your innate qualities and knowledge of your true nature and of higher realities.

Contemplate the words of many inspired individuals who have examined higher realities and shared their insights and personal discoveries.

Live enjoyably, compassionately, and skillfully with permanent Self-realization as your major aim in your current incarnation.

With warm best wishes and constant blessings,

Roy Eugene Davis

Autumn 2013
Lakemont, Georgia
U. S. A.

Roy Eugene Davis, founder and spiritual director of Center for Spiritual Awareness, has taught spiritual growth practices for more than six decades in North and South America, Japan, Europe, West Africa, and India. He was ordained by Paramahansa Yogananda in 1951.

INTRODUCTION

Knowing God

The word *God* has been widely used by adherents of monotheistic philosophical and religious systems to indicate one ultimate Reality or a concept of it. The oldest ancestor word from which it is thought to be derived is Sanskrit *hu*, used to "invoke or request" the presence or assistance and support of cosmic forces or the imagined deities which controlled them. In more recent times the word is thought to be related to an Anglo-Saxon word used in a German manuscript in the 6th century. The word *God* is not in Judeo-Christian scriptures written in Hebrew, Aramaic, Greek, or Latin, or in older religious texts in India or other parts of the world.

Some names used for ultimate Reality are: German *Gott*; Swedish *Gud*; Portuguese *Deus*; French *Dieu*; Italian *Dio*; Spanish *Dios*; Arabic *Allah*; Sanskrit *Brahman* for the transcendent aspect and *Ishwara* for an aspect thought to control cosmic forces; English *God*, *Lord*, *Heavenly Father*. *Divine Mother* is used to refer to intelligence-directed cosmic energy expressing as and in nature. Words used to indicate characteristics of ultimate Reality are omnipotence, *all power*; omniscience, *all knowing*; and omnipresence, *everywhere existing*.

Some people imagine God as a cosmic, human-like being with supernatural powers who cares about people, confers or withholds blessings, and saves some souls from suffering and misfortune. To others, God is a mystery to be eventually known, or perhaps can never be known.

Sequential Processes of Cosmic Manifestation

Transcendent, Absolute (Pure) Reality
Infinite (without boundaries), devoid of attributes.

Expressive Field With Three Constituent Attributes

luminosity	transformative influence	inertia
(sattwa)	(rajas)	(tamas)

Field of Primordial Nature
Om with time, space, and fine cosmic forces.

Field of Cosmic Mind
Field of individualized units of pure consciousness produced by the blending of the expressive field and the characteristics of the field of primordial nature. Souls have Self-awareness, intellect, mind, and ego (a confined sense of self-identity).

Causal Realm
Cosmic electromagnetic field and electromagnetic fields of souls. Abode of souls that have transcended the astral realm.

Astral Realm
Capacities to smell, taste, touch, hear, and see. Capacities of generation, excretion, mobility, manual dexterity, and speech. Five subtle element-essences. Abode of unenlightened souls after physical life.

Physical Universe
Material manifestations of five subtle element essences: space with fine substances; air, gaseous substances; fire, transformative; water, circulates, lubricates, and dissolves; earth, subatomic particles and atoms bonded by electromagnetic forces that form material things. Abode of souls incarnated in physical bodies.

In this book, the word God is used as a synonym for an ultimate Reality with a transcendent, pure essence and an expressive aspect with attributes that make possible the production and maintenance of universes.

The chart on the facing page illustrates processes of cosmic manifestation that emanate from the expressive field of ultimate Reality through fine and subtle stages to the physical realm in which we now exist. Look at the chart from time to time. As spiritual growth progresses and your innate knowledge is revealed, you will understand that the transcendent, pure essence of ultimate Reality is outside of space and time while the expressive aspect produces objective conditions.

Souls, units of the pure essence of ultimate Reality individualized in the field* of primordial nature, become further involved with objective manifestation in the field of cosmic mind. Souls are immortal, just as the pure essence of ultimate Reality of which they are units did not have an origin and will never cease to exist.

We have within us all knowledge of ultimate Reality, which is gradually or quickly unveiled or exposed as our awareness is clarified.

Spiritual enlightenment is Self-revelation.

*In the study of physics—the scientific investigation of matter and energy and of interactions between them—a *field* is defined as a region of space marked by a physical property, such as a gravitational or electromagnetic force.

PARAMAHANSA YOGANANDA 1893 – 1952
Guru of Roy Eugene Davis

God! God! God!

From the depths of slumber,
As I ascend the spiral stairways of wakefulness,
I will whisper: God! God! God!

Thou art the food, and when I break my fast
Of nightly separation from Thee,
I will taste Thee, and mentally say:
God! God! God!

No matter where I go, the spotlight of my mind
Will ever keep turning on Thee,
And in the battle din of activity, my silent war-cry
will be:
God! God! God!

When boisterous storms of trials shriek,
And when worries howl at me,
I will drown their clamor, loudly chanting
God! God! God!

When my mind weaves dreams
With threads of memories,
Then on that magic cloth will I emboss:
God! God! God!

Every night, in times of deepest sleep,
My peace dreams and calls, Joy! Joy! Joy!
And my joy comes singing evermore:
God! God! God!

In waking, eating, working, dreaming, sleeping,
Serving, meditating, chanting, divinely loving,
My soul will constantly hum, unheard by any:
God! God! God!

Swami [Paramahansa] Yogananda
From his book *Whispers From Eternity*; 1929.

Paramahansa Yogananda (right) with his guru
Swami Sri Yukteswar (1855 – 1936). *India, 1936*

JANUARY

January 1
Until we are enlightened, we see only the surface of our world; not the subtle attributes of nature, or that which produced them out of itself and sustains them. We need to know the truth about ourselves, our relationship with the Infinite, and how to live as we are meant to live.

January 2
Fervently aspire to be Self-realized. You will be inspired from the core of your essence of being and highly self-motivated to always experience and express excellence in all aspects of your life.

January 3
Intentional adherence to holistic* lifestyle regimens will empower you to be healthy, happy, optimistic, creatively expressive, and more spiritually conscious.

* **holistic** Emphasis on the whole and the interdependence of its parts. Our lifestyle is holistic when the spiritual, mental, emotional, physical, social, economic, and environmental components of our existence are harmonious integrated.

January 4
Attend to your spiritual practices. Improved powers of intellectual discrimination and intuition, orderly thinking, and sustained superconscious meditation practice allow spiritual growth to naturally occur.

Life has to be lived; why not live it the highest way?
– *Paramahansa Yogananda*

January 5
Acknowledge that you now have what you want or need. Affirmations can produce or attract constructive results when what is declared to be true is imagined as already actualized and elicits a feeling (awareness and conviction) of being true.

January 6
On the awakening path, we don't have to struggle to be spiritually conscious. The natural way is to cooperate with the awakening processes already occurring within us and learn to live with the full support of nature and freely provided impulses of grace.

January 7
Because we are individualized units of the pure essence of ultimate Reality, all knowledge of it that is within us is Self-revealed as it is allowed to emerge. When we are fully aware of ourselves as immortal, spiritual beings, our capacity to know ultimate Reality is limitless.

January 8
Ultimate Reality has an absolute (pure) essence outside of space and time and an expressive aspect with attributes which regulate cosmic forces which produce and maintain universes.

Affirm With Confidence
I am always receptive to new, worthwhile insights.

To every thing there is a season, and a time
to every purpose under the heaven; a time
to be born, and a time to die; a time to plant
and a time to harvest that which is planted.
– *Ecclesiastes 3:1,2*

January 9
All knowledge of processes of cosmic manifestation and our sojourn in space and time can be contemplated and fully "remembered."

January 10
The Om vibration expresses as primordial nature: time, space, and fine cosmic forces with potential to further manifest. It is the substance of everything in universes. Listen to Om in the stillness of meditation.

January 11
Primordial nature has two characteristics: it produces universes and blurs awareness of souls which are overly identified with it. Its processes are regulated by three constituent, energetic attributes of luminosity, transformation, and inertia.

January 12
Because you are a flawless unit of the pure essence of ultimate Reality, what is true of it must be true of you. Instead of thinking that you are separate from ultimate Reality, acknowledge the truth of what you are—now.

Affirm With Decisiveness
I am an immortal spiritual being, a flawless
unit of the pure essence of ultimate Reality.
The knowledge that I have, I lovingly
wish for everyone, everywhere.

Lead me from the unreal to the real! Lead me from darkness to light! Lead me from [belief in] death to [realization of] immortality!
– *The Brihadaranyaka Upanishad*

January 13

Quickly grow to emotional maturity. A characteristic of emotional maturity is willingness to be responsible for mental attitudes, emotions, personal behaviors, and the results of our random or intentional actions.

January 14

Aspire to be so spiritually aware that the purity of your essence of being constantly illumines your mind and consciousness, vitalizes your body, and blesses everyone who is influenced by your mental states, states of consciousness, and actions.

January 15

The final solution to all human problems is spiritual enlightenment: complete knowledge of our true nature and of ultimate Reality.

January 16

Higher realities can be partially known by intellectual inquiry; better known by using intuition; and accurately known by direct experience.

Affirm With Conviction
In the deep silence of daily meditation
I become increasingly aware of my
true nature and relationship
with the Infinite.

The necessity of an inward silence
has appeared clearly to my mind.
– *John Woolman (1720 – 1772)*

January 17
Although we need to relate to everyday circumstances and live effectively, for our complete well-being we need to have knowledge of higher realities that replaces all erroneous ideas.

January 18
Do we know what is real, authentic, or actual, or are we inclined to agree with ideas and opinions that others express? Prefer the freedom and deep soul-satisfaction of personal discovery of what is true.

January 19
As temporary sojourners in the sea of life, we are fated to wander in space and time and experience a variety of relationships and circumstances until we awaken from the dream of mortality and fulfill our spiritual destiny.

January 20
We experience lingering effects of mental conditionings and personal actions because of clouded awareness and conflicted mental and emotional states. Think constructively, act wisely, clarify your awareness, and heal and rise above troubled mental and emotional states.

Affirm With Decisive Intention
I am quickly awakening to flawless experience
and knowledge of my immortal, true nature.

I absorbed my attention within
and realized my true Self.
– *Kabir (1440 – 1518)*

January 21
To be fulfilled we need to be in harmonious accord with the processes of nature, have our life-enhancing desires easily fulfilled, have needs spontaneously satisfied, and experience rapid spiritual growth that will culminate in illumination of consciousness.

January 22
To mistake the unreal for the Real (that which endures) is a primary intellectual error that results in irrational thinking and purposeless behaviors. Preoccupation with transient phenomena should be avoided. Attention and actions should be concentrated on holistic living and nurturing spiritual growth.

January 23
Sincere aspiration to be spiritually enlightened, wisely chosen personal behaviors, and cooperation with our innate urge to have awareness restored to wholeness can allow spiritual growth to occur more easily and faster.

January 24
Are all of our purposes of real value? Superficial thinking, relationships, and activities are not soul-satisfying. We need to inquire: When I have completed my projects, satisfied my desires, and fulfilled my commitments, will all of my actions have been worthwhile?

Affirm With Conviction
I always live with clear awareness of useful
soul-satisfying aims and purposes.

The true Self is never born, nor does it ever die.
The true Self is permanent and ageless.
– *Bhagavad Gita 2:20*

January 25
A life that is not skillfully lived with clear awareness of meaningful purposes is almost entirely wasted because authentic spiritual growth—the primary purpose for our being in this world—is neglected.

January 26
When we know how to live, are sustained by faith, and motivated and energized by Self-confident will to excel, we can redeem the troubled past and serenely anticipate the continuous emergence of good fortune.

January 27
When we are Self-confident it is easy to be enthusiastic, enjoyable to imagine desired outcomes of plans and actions, rewarding to see through appearances of discord to harmonious possibilities that can be actualized, pleasant to accept good fortune that is immediately available, and natural to have our highest good actualized by our concentrated intentions, effective actions, and freely expressive grace.

January 28
We can discover the best way to live by effectively using our knowledge and skills, imagining worthwhile possibilities, engaging in meaningful endeavors, and being alert and responsive to unplanned life-enhancing events and situations that are provided for us.

Affirm With Confidence
I faithfully attend to my spiritual practices and am thankful for the positive results that I have.

He who sees the Infinite in all things sees God.
– *William Blake (1757 – 1827)*

January 29
The work we do, service we render, or actions we perform that produce constructive results are beneficial to us and to others. When our relationships with the universe are harmonious, it can more readily provide resources and supportive events, circumstances, and relationships for our highest good.

January 30
We should always expect the highest good for ourselves and for others. Expectations impressed into the cosmic mind can be expressed as objective circumstances.

January 31
A mistaken sense of self-identity is the primary obstacle to spiritual awakening. When that error in perception is corrected, our awareness is immediately restored to its original, pure wholeness.

Affirm With Gratitude
The constantly expressive, radiant purity of my essence of being that illumines my mind and consciousness also improves my powers of perception, refines my nervous system, and progressively develops the capacities of my brain to accommodate superconscious and cosmic conscious realizations.

Whatever you desire with intense concentration, the universe will manfest for you.
– *Swami Sri Yukteswar*

Meditate Daily

There is a quiet place within you to which you can retire whenever you want or need to experience perfect peace and wholeness. Rest in conscious awareness of your true nature every day as you meditate in God.

- Sit upright. Close your eyes. Put your attention in the front and higher region of your brain. Pray silently or sit quietly. Know that you are a spiritual being in the wholeness of God's presence.
- When meditation flows spontaneously, let it happen. If it doesn't flow easily, use a meditation technique to calm the mind: pray, observe your breathing, listen to a chosen word or word-phrase (mantra), or use any helpful method. Don't be anxious about the outcome. Avoid extreme effort. Be alert and attentive.
- When you are poised and tranquil, rest in that calm, clear state until you conclude the session. Retain your meditative calm as you resume your activities.

Meditate once or twice a day for 15 to 20 minutes to refresh the mind, improve overall health, and facilitate natural spiritual growth. Meditate longer to experience deep soul-silence. If you are a new meditator, you will be more proficient with regular practice.

An Enlivening Power is Nurturing the Universe
and We Can Learn to Cooperate With It

In the Center for Spiritual Awareness Meditation Hall. White marble statues of Babaji, Lahiri Mahasaya, Sri Yukteswar, and Paramahansa Yogananda were made by artisans in Jaipur, India.

FEBRUARY

February 1
Spiritual growth can occur naturally when we live in harmony with nature's laws, improve our powers of perception, and nurture superconsciousness.

February 2
To have your awareness restored to wholeness, discern the difference between your permanent pure-conscious essence and fragmented states of awareness produced by excessive identification with mental states, emotions, and objective conditions.

February 3
When you are calmly established in Self-awareness, you can effectively live with insightful understanding.

February 4
Conditions that modify awareness and interfere with spiritual growth can be resisted and neutralized by constructive thinking and living, and superconscious meditation practice.

February 5
Supplemental practices that can reveal our true nature include having faith, sincere right endeavor to facilitate spiritual growth, improving intellectual and intuitive abilities, and wholesome lifestyle routines that improve overall health and vitality.

Every day, meditate more deeply
than you did the day before.
– *Paramahansa Yogananda*

February 6
Mastery of attention is necessary for rational thinking, focused concentration, purposeful living, and enjoyable meditation practice.

February 7
For harmonious relationships and psychological health, cultivate harmlessness, truthfulness, honesty, conservation of vital force, and generosity.

February 8
Learn to calmly observe thoughts that rise and fall in your mind, perceptions flowing through your awareness, and events that emerge and fade in space and time.

February 9
Be true to your real Self, which is always pure, serene, whole, and enlightened.

February 10
It is natural to be honest in relationships when we are true to ourselves and know that our thoughts, states of consciousness, and actions determine our experiences.

Affirm With Sincerity
I am completely dedicated to wholesome living,
constructive thinking, compassionate relationships,
and effective spiritual practices.

Restless thoughts are caused
by restless vital forces.
– *Lahiri Mahasaya (1828 – 1895)*
Guru of Swami Sri Yukteswar

February 11
Worry, stress, restlessness, confusion, emotional unrest, useless talking, addictive behaviors, insufficient rest, and excessive sensory stimulation dissipate vital forces, weaken the mind, and blur soul awareness. Faith, optimism, sufficient rest, emotional calmness, decisiveness, wholesome behaviors, balanced schedules of activity and rest, and regular interludes of meditation energize the mind, vitalize the body, and clarify our awareness.

February 12
A natural law is a principle that is the same in all circumstances. Learn the spiritual, mental, and physical laws of cause and effect and cooperate with them.

February 13
Observe physical and environmental cleanliness; cultivate soul-contentment in all circumstances; wisely control mental states, emotions, and behaviors; profoundly study higher realities; see beyond mistaken perceptions of self-identity.

February 14
Mental purity and purity of motives and intentions are as important as physical and environmental cleanliness.

February 15
Learn to always be aware of existing in one, ultimate Reality without boundaries or limits.

One whose mind is disciplined, whose senses are well-regulated, who is free from attachments and aversions, is tranquil. That purity of spirit removes all sorrows. Knowledge is [then] soon settled in permanent peace.
– *Bhagavad Gita 2:64,65*

February 16
Psychological conflict inhibits spiritual growth. To allow spiritual growth to be easier, remove mental conditionings and avoid emotional conflicts that interfere with it. As soul awareness increases, superconscious influences can complete the transformation processes.

February 17
Constantly acknowledge your divine nature as you live creatively with knowledge-directed purpose. View your life in the physical realm as an opportunity to learn all there is to know about your true nature, the universe, and what is beyond what is ordinarily seen.

February 18
A mistaken sense of self-identity is caused by a lack of spiritual awareness. When small, self-centered ideas and feelings are discarded, pure awareness remains.

February 19
After an interlude of quiet meditation, go deeper in the silence until you are conscious of a Presence around and through you. Then aspire to go beyond that to its pure essence.

Disciplined thinking and actions, profound study of higher realities, and surrendering [letting go of] one's mistaken sense of self-identity to experience pure consciousness are the disciplines of Kriya Yoga. Kriya Yoga is practiced to resist, weaken, and remove restrictive influences and cultivate Self- and God-realization.
– *Patanjali's Yoga-Sutra 2:1,2*

February 20
Spiritual enlightenment isn't a travel-destination or a state of consciousness to be attained. It is experience of our pure nature that has in it all knowledge of higher realities. Aspire to be fully awake.

February 21
A mind without illusions can function rationally, process perceptions, and accommodate innate knowledge as it is unveiled. Flawless Self-knowledge completely illumines our mind and consciousness.

February 22
When we are inclined to be impulsive or allow troublesome habits to influence our moods and behaviors, we should act wisely and decisively.

February 23
Unwanted circumstances can be patiently endured until they are changed. Be patient by being soul-centered, mentally peaceful, emotionally calm, and discerning in all situations and relationships.

February 24
Until we are Self-realized, we should adopt the constructive mental attitudes and emulate the behaviors that Self-realized people naturally express.

By deep meditation and right living, calm the waves of thoughts and desires that cause ordinary perceptions of reality. Then superconscious, you will behold everything as it really is.
– *Paramahansa Yogananda*

February 25
Cultivate constructive mental attitudes, emotions, lifestyle routines, behaviors, environmental conditions, and relationships that enhance your life and quicken your spiritual awakening.

February 26
When we are established in Self-knowledge, conflicting philosophical opinions or theories don't disturb our mental peace. When intellectual and intuitive powers are highly developed, subtle truths are easily discerned.

February 27
Appropriate actions of Self-realized people are impelled from their essence of being. With understanding of life's wholeness, they are constantly nurtured and supported by the inexhaustible Source of everything.

February 28
Our aspiration to be spiritually enlightened should be unwavering, reinforced by mental attitudes and actions that allow spiritual growth to effortlessly occur.

February 29 (During a Leap Year)
When you meditate, be fully attentive to the purpose of practice, then be fully alert when you are again engaged in purposeful endeavors.

This is the noble truth of the way that leads
to the stopping of sorrow. It is the noble eightfold
path: right views, right aspirations, right speech,
right conduct, right livelihood, right endeavor,
right mindfulness, and right contemplation.
– *The teachings of the Buddha / The Pali Canon*

How to Use Affirmations Effectively

Affirmations are audible or mental declarations of what is true or what you want to be true for you. They should be concise and clearly defined. Don't try to condition the mind or indulge in fantasy. Affirm with intention until you have conviction of having what you want or need. What you definitely "have" in your consciousness, can be produced by or attracted to you.

1. Acknowledge your innate divine nature and Presence of God in and around you.
2. Audibly speak the affirmation with intention two or three times, quietly two or three times, very quietly two or three times, then mentally a few times. Feel and imagine that *you have* what you affirm.

If you affirm having a positive mental attitude or being cheerful, optimistic, inspired, self-confident, and highly motivated, results can be immediate.

If you affirm physical health and well-being, you can immediately feel more energetic even though you may also need to adopt holistic lifestyle regimens and other practices to assist healing processes.

For success in endeavors, nurture positive thoughts and feelings while performing effective actions. Remember that your mind is a unit of cosmic mind which is inclined to respond to your desires, needs, intentions, and expectations.

JAMES J. LYNN 1892 – 1955
Disciple of Paramahansa Yogananda

MARCH

March 1
If we don't have a clear idea of what God is when we begin on the spiritual path, when we sincerely endeavor to live righteously and engage in spiritual practices, the reality of God will be revealed.

March 2
To be healthy, happy, and in the flow of good fortune, we need to be spiritually awake and in harmony with the rhythms of life. Passive or confused wishful thinking or erratic behaviors cannot produce or attract results we want to have.

March 3
To accomplish meaningful purposes, *imagine* them to be already accomplished. *Feel* as you will feel when they are accomplished. It will then be easier to constructively think and act.

March 4
Clearly defined purposes attune our mind with cosmic mind (which is responsive to desires, needs, intentions, and expectations) and attract supportive influences.

March 5
If habits of thinking and behaving need to be improved, now is the time to adopt new, constructive habits.

Deep within us all there is an amazing inner sanctuary of the soul, a holy place, a Divine Center.
– *Thomas R. Kelly (1893 – 1941)*

March 6
Absolute liberation of consciousness is the ideal of the aspirant who is committed to a spiritual path. People with weak or inconstant resolve are inclined to be satisfied with limited freedom which provides only a degree of temporary comfort. Resolve to be fully awake.

March 7
Pessimists generate unhappiness by nurturing thoughts and feelings of sadness and despair. Optimists always see abundant good fortune that is possible to have and are happy, enthusiastic, and energetic.

March 8
Because the reality of God is always fully present where we are, we can be Self-realized, healthy, affluent, freely expressive, and fulfilled in this world.

March 9
This world is our temporary abode. Our true origin is pure Consciousness-Existence from which we emerged into the realm of nature and to which we will return. Awakening to Self-knowledge may be slow, fast, or very fast according to our capacity to accommodate it and the intensiveness of our right spiritual practices.

Affirm With Realization
I truly know and clearly see the reality of
God always fully present where I am.

Read a little; meditate more;
think of God all the time
– *Paramahansa Yogananda*

March 10
Regular, proficient superconscious meditation practice accelerates our spiritual growth and allows impulses of grace from deep within us to be transformational.

March 11
The key to effective meditation is to practice with alert attention. Short sessions elicit relaxation and mental calm, provide physical and psychological benefits, and contribute to gradual spiritual growth. Longer, deeper meditation clarifies awareness and reveals our innate qualities and Self-knowledge. Meditate alertly.

March 12
When meditating, physical sensations, thoughts, moods, and memories should be ignored. Aspire to awaken to levels of awareness that are not dependent upon objects of perception—thoughts, visual perceptions, or feelings. Be satisfied only with Self-realization.

March 13
There will never be a better time than now to make, or renew, your commitment to right living and spiritual growth. You are an immortal being destined to awaken in God. If you sincerely want to, you can be Self-realized and liberated in one incarnation.

March 14
Heed the counsel of enlightened people. Be inspired by the example of their lives and highly Self-motivated to be fully spiritually enlightened.

Affirm With Sincerity
I am completely dedicated to my spiritual path.

March 15
Because the reality of God is present where we are, we can have complete personal fulfillment here and now. If we are not yet spiritually enlightened, we have only to be more conscious.

March 16
When you are aware of the erroneous beliefs or opinions that you have acquired or assumed regarding mundane matters or philosophical ideas, renounce them. You will feel lighter. Your mind will be more clear and you will be emotionally peaceful and happy.

March 17
Inspiration arouses creative imagination, empowers us to think and act constructively, vitalizes the mind and body, awakens intuition, and impels us to experience and express excellence in all aspects of life.

March 18
Inspiration removes mental dullness and confusion and provides glimpses of transcendent realities. Nurture inspiration with optimism, prayer, meditation, and attentive practice of the presence of God.

March 19
View yourself as an immortal spiritual being: healthy-minded, problem-free, functionally effective, prosperous, and successful.

If happiness is activity in accordance with
excellence, it is reasonable that it should be
in accordance with the highest excellence.
– *Aristotle (384 – 322 B.C.E.)*

March 20
Don't be so obsessed with formal practice of spiritual exercises that you neglect everyday duties, nor be so compulsive about satisfying desires and accomplishing personal purposes that you neglect to be Self- and God-aware. Without clear Self- and God-awareness, life is superficial and unsatisfying.

March 21
Whatever you can vividly imagine, ardently believe, and comfortably accept as being possible for you to have or experience, can be manifested in your life. Through your mind, you interact with Universal Mind which produces or makes possible what you habitually think about and are receptive to having and experiencing.

March 22
Outgrow the idea that God is a cosmic parent-figure, that you are separate from God, and all other limiting beliefs. Learn to perceive accurately to avoid illusions which cloud awareness and interfere with rational thinking. Be willing to grow to emotional maturity: to be responsible for your well-being, choices, and actions. Be anchored in God-realization.

Affirm With Conviction
I am responsible for my well-being, choices,
decisions, actions, and circumstances.

Manifest plainness,
Embrace Simplicity
Reduce Selfishness,
Have few desires.
– *Lao-tzu (604 – 531 B.C.E.)*

March 23
Discard thoughts, behaviors, relationships, and actions which are incompatible with your highest ideals. Whatever concept of the ideal life you have, actualize it now. Don't wait to make useful changes.

March 24
Once resolved on a constructive course of action, persist until you have the results. Go deeper into God while faithfully continuing to do what is useful.

March 25
The mistaken belief that a separation exists between us and God can result in irrational thinking, psychological conflicts, purposeless behaviors, and unsatisfying spiritual growth. Acknowledge your oneness with God.

March 26
When we are Self-realized our inner light radiates to others and to the world; our mental peace is a calming influence; our intentional behaviors are productive.

Affirm With Conviction
I never allow false ideas to distort my mind or illusions to blur my awareness. I always think rationally and perceive flawlessly.

You are told that you should love your neighbor as yourself; but if you love yourself meanly, childishly, timidly, even so shall you love your neighbor. Learn to love yourself with a love that is wise and healthy, that is large and complete.

– *Maurice Maeterlinck (1862 – 1949)*
Wisdom and Destiny

March 27
See through outer appearances and behaviors of others. Silently acknowledge and respect their divine essence.

March 28
Generous, appropriate giving prospers us by enabling us to be aware of the wholeness of life. See needs and fill them. See hurts and heal them.

March 29
When we are receptive to life, it can more easily provide us with what we want or need. Renounce thoughts of limitation. Maintain mental attitudes—and feelings—of freedom and abundance.

March 30
Don't withhold your good will and kind thoughts. Be thankful when you learn of the good fortune of others and wish for good fortune for everyone.

March 31
We don't have to try to find God because God is not hidden. We don't have to try to establish a connection with God because God exists within and around us. The God-union of which mystics speak is the apprehension and vivid experience of our existing oneness.

Affirm With Confidence
I am aware of the Presence and reality of God.

The things that we see about us are God's thoughts and words to us; and if we were but wise there is not a step that we take which we should not find to be full of mighty instruction.
— *Charles Haddon Spurgeon (1834 – 1892)*

J. OLIVER BLACK 1893 – 1989
Disciple of Paramahansa Yogananda

APRIL

April 1
There are many helpful things we can do to remove our awareness from the restless mind and surging senses. The final freedom is due to God's grace.

April 2
God's grace expresses from within us because there is no separation between us and God. Grace expresses around us because God is all-pervading. God's grace causes our spontaneous spiritual unfoldments, the unplanned and unanticipated supportive events and circumstances we frequently experience, and the final removal of delusion (unknowing) from our awareness.

April 3
The highest knowledge enables us to know the truth about life and to view circumstances with equanimity. Thus established in Self-realization, our highest good is revealed and there is nothing more to which to aspire.

April 4
Our progress in spiritual growth can be accurately determined by observation of our mental and emotional states and functional behaviors. If we are always mentally calm; emotionally stable; cheerfully willing to be responsible for our thoughts, moods, and behaviors; and attentive to duties and purposes, our soul qualities are effectively actualized.

Affirm With Conviction
My thoughts and actions are always constructive.

April 5
In the midst of chosen or necessary duties and activities, we may forget that our most important duty is to always be awake in God. When our soul qualities are actualized we can be healthy-minded, creatively functional, and of real value to society.

April 6
Do your best to think, feel, and live in accord with your highest understanding. Meditate every day to the stage of tranquil, thought-free awareness.

April 7
Imagine and intuitively glimpse what is possible for you to ultimately know and experience, then learn how to be receptive to realizing it.

April 8
Acquire accurate information from reliable sources, then use your intelligence and common sense to discern what is true.

April 9
Some causes of resistance to learning new ideas and behaviors are egotism, apathy, uncertainty, fear of the unknown, and attachment to habitual mental attitudes and personality characteristics. Be willing to learn.

Affirm With Conviction
I faithfully persist on my spiritual awakening path.

When the purity of the Self [true nature],
mind, intellect, and awareness is the same,
absolute Self-realization prevails.
– *Patanjali's Yoga-Sutra 3:56*

April 10
Egotism, an inflated sense of self-importance expressed as arrogance, is nurtured by feelings of insecurity. With Self-understanding egotism is replaced with humility.

April 11
Awareness, ego (a mistaken sense of self-identity), the faculty of intellect, and a mind are the four components of individualized consciousness. Discern the difference between the real you as an aware observer and the ego, intellect, and mental states.

April 12
Avoid inclinations to want to create a strong, artificial sense of personality-based self-esteem. It is much more spiritually beneficial to be Self-realized.

April 13
Self- and God-realization is naturally present when you are fully conscious of your essence of being. Aspire to be fully conscious.

April 14
Healthy long life has great value because it provides us with enough time to awaken to Self- and God-realization in our current incarnation.

The mind generates countless ideas which weaken it and veil perceptions of truth. These cause impressions and tendencies in the mind which are, for the most part, latent or dormant. When the mind is rid of them, the veil vanishes in a moment like mist at sunrise, and with it the greatest of sorrows.
– *Vasishta's Yoga*

April 15
Be inspired from the depths of your being rather than dependent on random thoughts, changing moods, or the encouragement of others. The Reality that illumines the minds of saints is within you.

April 16
Debilitating habits and unwise choices of activities and relationships blur awareness and interfere with orderly spiritual growth. Live wisely with conscious intention.

April 17
Endeavors to attempt to create enduring monuments to glorify ourselves are misdirected and doomed to failure. Let the results of wisely performed, constructive actions be your selfless service to the universe and life.

April 18
In the darkest of our dark nights, the inner light ever shines. To know that God is the reality of our lives is to know that regardless of conditions which may challenge us, our highest good is assured. The Intelligence-Power that produced the worlds is superior to any situation.

Affirm with Realization
I am always Self- and God-aware
while creatively thriving in all
useful endeavors.

You are on Earth for but a little while, and your
real reason for being here is very different from
what you may have imagined.
– *Paramahansa Yogananda*

April 19
Transitory events and circumstances are appearances on the screen of space-time. Their supporting causes can be changed by right understanding and skillful actions. The flowing processes of life are always changing.

April 20
All prophets of doom are intellectually incompetent or emotionally disturbed. They don't know or are incapable of comprehending the trends of evolution that transform nature and nurture the spiritual awakening of souls.

April 21
We cannot forever ignore our own divine essence. While we may play with fleeting thoughts or feelings or try to cling to a fragile sense of independent self-identity, at a deeper level we are free and blissful. Acknowledge your true Self and let it emerge.

April 22
Don't say that you don't have time to nurture spiritual growth. Where you are, doing what you are doing, is the place and time to be conscious of your real nature and relationship with the Infinite.

Affirm With Realization
I joyously acknowledge my immortal essence of being.

When the waves of consciousness are transcended by concentrated meditation, pure oneness with the supreme Self [God] is realized.
– *Lahiri Mahasaya*

April 23
How can your life to be more meaningful for you and for others? Write the thoughts and plans that arise in your mind. Follow through with helpful actions.

April 24
The ongoing processes of life are always providing many opportunities for you to experience your highest good. Look for them, and make wise choices.

April 25
When you know what is best for you, don't be afraid or ashamed to calmly ask the universe to help you produce or attract it.

April 26
Be a possibility-thinker. After an interlude of tranquil meditation, open your mind to "what can be so" for you. Think of practical ways to help yourself. You will have helpful insights and ideas. Supportive events and timely circumstances will emerge.

April 27
Daily contemplate the truth of your innermost level of being and the reality of God. You can be fully awake in God and live joyously in tune with the Infinite.

April 28
Your choices and actions of the moment determine your near and distant future experiences. Choose wisely and act decisively. Your highest good is available to you.

Affirm With Enthusiasm
I always think wisely and act decisively.

April 29
The redemptive results of alert meditative contemplation are experienced when we are firmly established in Self- and God-realization.

April 30
When we didn't know the inner truth about ourselves we may have been inclined to make mistakes. Now that we know we are spiritual beings abiding in God, we cannot pretend that we don't know about our relationship with the Infinite. We have to assume responsibility for wisely chosen constructive use of our knowledge, abilities, and resources.

Affirm With Realization
I am always healthy, happy, and radiantly alive!
I am always constructively inspired and Self-motivated!
I can skillfully do the things I want or need to do!
My mental powers are constantly strong and reliable!
My intellectual abilities are rapidly improving!
I daily meditate, easily, naturally, and enjoyably!

To define yourself in terms of human limitations
is a desecration of the image of God you are.
– *Paramahansa Yogananda*

FAYE WRIGHT (DAYA MATA) 1914 – 2010
Disciple of Paramahansa Yogananda

MAY

May 1
When you have sincerely done everything you could do to accomplish a purpose, achieve a goal, solve a problem, or overcome a troublesome situation, remove your attention from external conditions. Trust God and nature's processes to do what you could not do.

May 2
The more you yield to your innate urge to be unconfined and expressive, the greater will be your happiness and freedom. You are destined to be fully conscious of your true nature and eternal relationship with the Infinite.

May 3
The mind is constantly being impressed by thoughts and perceptions. Allow it to also be frequently influenced by meditative, superconscious realizations.

May 4
After meditation, sit calmly for a few minutes. Let your superconscious awareness pervade your mind and body. Acknowledge all souls in the universe and wish for their total well-being and spiritual fulfillment. Continue until you are established in awareness of wholeness.

Affirm With Realization
The radiant purity of my essence of being beneficially influences everyone and all forms and processes of life.

Thinking that you are not free keeps you from being free. Stop thinking like that and you will be free.
– *Paramahansa Yogananda*

May 5
When our perceptions are flawless, we can be aware of the expressive attributes of ultimate Reality that produced and maintains the universe.

May 6
Spontaneous insights about ourselves, life, and higher realities can often pleasantly surprise us. Be alert and attentive, prepared for those moments of discovery.

May 7
Be higher purpose-directed by thinking constructively, wisely acting with decisive intention, and rapidly growing to emotional and spiritual maturity.

May 8
Nothing external to ourselves can bless or deprive us. Our states of consciousness, mental states, and habitual behaviors determine our experiences. By living effectively, we can experience continuous good fortune.

Affirm With Realization
I am always Self-aware, think constructively, live effectively, and experience continuous good fortune.

Discard the false belief that there is a separation between spiritual and material life. All constructive work is purifying when done with the right motive. If you sometimes fail to accomplish your purposes, don't be discouraged or defeated. That is the best time to sow seeds of success. In everything that you do, express your limitless soul qualities.
– *Paramahansa Yogananda*

May 9
Frustration, anger, fear, worry, pessimism, moodiness, egocentricity, and other debilitating conditions can be quickly removed when our perception of our essence of being is accurate.

May 10
We don't have to be cloistered to grow spiritually. When our lifestyle is wholesome, duties are properly fulfilled, actions are performed without attachment to them or their results, and effective spiritual practices are maintained, progressive awakening easily occurs.

May 11
Four prerequisites for success on the discipleship path are: intelligence to comprehend what is to be learned; renunciation of erroneous ideas and addictive and self-defeating behaviors; ethical living; and firm resolve to be permanently spiritually enlightened.

May 12
Learning, reflection, and meditation are fundamental discipleship practices. What is learned should be contemplated until it is fully comprehended. Superconscious meditation should be faithfully practiced until consciousness is restored its original, pure wholeness

Affirm With Gratitude
I am quickly awakening to Self- and God-realization.

By practicing meditation as advised by one's guru [teacher] the sound of Om can be heard. Breathing is then regulated and physical aging is slowed.
– *Swami Sri Yukteswar*

May 13
It is easy to know what we consider to be of greatest value. What do we think about most of the time? What do we desire above all else? To what do we primarily direct our attention, energies, actions, and resources?

May 14
Only Self- and God-realization can fully satisfy our innate urge to be completely fulfilled. Awaken to Self- and God-realization as quickly as possible.

May 15
Whatever you think—or imagine—God to be, that idea can be the beginning of your relationship with God. As your understanding improves, you will discover that God is not what you thought or imagined.

May 16
That which originated your involvement with the realm of nature has sustained and provided for you until now and will continue to do so. Trust it.

May 17
When we say it is human nature to behave in certain ways, we are acknowledging that acquired or instinctive modes of behavior are often characteristic of us and of others whom we know. While observing the human condition, we can also be aware of our divine nature. We can live with Self-determined intention rather than as creatures of habit or circumstances.

Affirm With Thankfulness
I joyously welcome each new day.

May 18
Overcome misfortune such as illness, accidents, personality conflicts, financial difficulty, or other troublesome conditions and live skillfully to avoid them in the future.

May 19
Some common causes of personal misfortune are lack of knowledge of how to think and act constructively; habitual thinking and behaviors that produce or attract misfortune; self-centered thinking and behaviors; irrational, confused thinking; inattentiveness; and believing that difficulties are normal conditions. Creatively actualize ideal possibilities.

May 20
When having difficulty relating to another person, try to improve your communication while remaining calm and radiating good will.

May 21
At all times, be Self-aware and think and act rationally. Misfortune can be avoided by having conviction that it is not possible for you to experience any condition that is not harmonious and constructive.

May 22
The primary cause of problems is insufficient spiritual awareness and understanding. When awareness and knowledge of our true nature is lacking, we may think of ourselves as mere human creatures. The final solution to all problems is spiritual awakening that removes our awareness from all illusions (misperceptions).

May 23
Discern the difference between your essence (true Self) and objective and subjective conditions. Live gracefully with flawless understanding.

May 24
A circumstance or event is an actualization of its cause. Whether we are aware of it or not, our habitual mental states and actions are always influencing our circumstances and experiences.

May 25
Even though we endeavor to perform actions to produce desired effects, if we harbor thoughts and expectations to the contrary, we may attract corresponding circumstances or unconsciously perform actions that thwart our purposes. Live with conscious intention.

May 26
Some people have psychological problems and distorted perceptions of themselves and their world because they think and feel that they are "only human" instead of aspiring to be spiritually consciousness. Refuse to think in terms of limitation.

May 27
Be committed to right living and spiritual practices that clarify your awareness, allow your innate divine qualities to emerge, and improve your capacities to be spiritually enlightened.

Better than rulership over the worlds ...
is the reward of the first step in holiness.
– *Words of the Doctrine (Buddhist Text)*

May 28
To make spiritual growth easier, cultivate awareness of God, live in accord with your highest understanding, and frequently meditate long and deep in the silence.

May 29
In meditative silence, rest in knowledge and awareness of yourself as a spiritual being. Sit for as long as necessary until a change of awareness occurs.

May 30
Rest in meditative silence until thoughts and feelings are quieted and you are alone in the Infinite. When poised in Self-realization, live skillfully and effectively.

May 31
Ordinary (modified) consciousness is clouded by mental and emotional unrest, illusions, memories, and preoccupation with self-centered concerns. When those conditions are absent, our changeless, pure essence can be revealed.

Affirm With Conviction
I live constructively with unwavering faith and appropriate, skillful actions. With optimistic resolve I am steadfast on my spiritual awakening path.

In the light of the eternal we are manifest, and even this very passing instant pulsates with a life that is needed in all the worlds to express. In vain would we wander in darkness; we are eternally at home in God.
– *Josiah Royce (1855 – 1916)*

International Kriya Yoga Congress, San Jose, California. *March 2013*

JUNE

June 1
There is a difference between passive sympathy and active compassion. We may be aware of the discomfort of others without doing anything to ease their pain. We are truly compassionate when we actually help others in meaningful ways.

June 2
Compassionate, moral behavior is always nurturing and supportive. Think and act in ways that bless and uplift others and support all forms and processes of life.

June 3
Moral personal conduct is supportive of us, society, and nature. It keeps us in harmonious relationship with the universe and sustains our attunement with the Infinite.

June 4
Thoughtful behaviors nurture supportive personal relationships. As our soul qualities emerge, we are naturally inclined to think and behave appropriately.

Affirm With Sincerity
While awakening to Self- and God-realization,
I wish for, and see, the highest good for everyone.

Agape is a unique type of love … that pours
itself out regardless of merit … it floods out like
the sun to reach the just and the unjust.
– *Rufus Jones (1863 – 1948)*
Pathways to the Reality of God

June 5
We cannot have meaningful relationships with others until we are at peace within ourselves.

June 6
Self-knowledge reveals that all beings are units of the pure essence of ultimate Reality. We are then inclined to care about the welfare of all people and forms of life, and to want to assist them to their highest good.

June 7
Do you know someone who could benefit from your compassionate actions? What can you now do to help them? While charitable (loving) thoughts and prayers are supportive, appropriate actions may also be needed. Think about the real needs of people whom you know and do what you can to assist them to learn about, awaken to, and actualize their innate potential.

June 8
Examine your thoughts and feelings. Do you often think about limitations and feel confined and frustrated, or is it easy for you to think and know that, with God, your highest good is always possible? Thoughts and feelings reflect your states of consciousness and choices. Choose them wisely.

June 9
As flawless, immortal units of the pure essence of ultimate Reality, we are like bubbles in an infinite ocean of consciousness.

Affirm With Realization
I am increasingly aware of the limitless ocean of consciousness.

June 10
If we listen carefully, we can hear the universe asking: 'What do you want?" Then it informs: "If you choose it, I will provide it for you." What do *you* really want?

June 11
Choose to be spiritually conscious, freely functional, and always successful in your well-chosen endeavors.

June 12
Meditate by detaching attention from the senses and from mental activities while directing it inward to the essence of your being—your Self-sufficient pure nature which requires no external support.

June 13
Schedule private time every day to be alone in silence. Pray to invoke awareness of God's presence. If meditation flows spontaneously, be still and let superconsciousness emerge. Be attentive to the process. Let all sense of personal self-identity dissolve as awareness of your true Self as pure consciousness is revealed.

June 14
If meditation isn't effortless, use a technique to elicit relaxation, quiet the mind, and improve concentration. Observe the natural flow of breathing, mentally listen to your chosen word or mantra, or use any procedure you know to be helpful.

... I think now that everything without exception has an eternal soul—The trees have, rooted in the ground; the weeds of the sea have; the animals.
– *Walt Whitman (1819 – 1892)*
To Think of Time

June 15
In the early stages of meditation, be aware of your breathing rhythm. You may mentally recite a preferred mantra (word or word-phrase) when you inhale and exhale. When your attention is focused, mentally listen to the word without reciting it. When the mental sound of the word is subtle, discard it and rest in deep silence.

June 16
When meditating, having your attention and awareness in the front and higher region of your brain can enable you to concentrate better and avoid involvement with thoughts and subconscious influences.

June 17
Listen within to discern subtle sounds that arise in your field of awareness. Whatever sound you hear, gently endeavor to hear a more subtle sound behind it. Continue until the subtlest sound you hear is constant, and use it as your meditation mantra.

June 18
Presume the subtle, constant inner sound that you hear to be an aspect of Om vibration pervading the universe. Merge attention and awareness in it, and expand in it. Then go beyond Om to awaken to pure consciousness.

June 19
Meditation techniques are "tools" we use to accomplish a purpose. Use them skillfully, then put them aside.

> A yogi should steadfastly contemplate the Supreme Reality, in solitude, alone, with mind and body controlled, having no cravings for anything [else].
> — *Bhagavad Gita 6:10*

June 20

If you perceive light in the spiritual eye center, let your attention be attracted to it. When the mind is calm, clear white light may be perceived. Perceptions of forms and other visual phenomena produced by the mind should be ignored.

June 21

When meditating, if it seems that nothing worthwhile is being experienced, relax. Sit patiently, watching and waiting. Nothing else is more important than what you are doing. Learn to enjoy the silence.

June 22

When meditating, changeable perceptions that you have are not your real nature. Be satisfied only with Self-knowledge and God-realization.

June 23

Who you think you are is a temporary, inaccurate sense of self-identity. Inquire: "What am I?" until you discover your enduring essence.

June 24

When mental transformations cease, pure consciousness can be revealed and experienced. In deep meditation, be established in your essence.

Established in a comfortable, steady meditation
posture, in a clean, appropriate place; there, intent
on practice, with thoughts and senses controlled,
the yogi should meditate to purify the mind.
– *Bhagavad Gita 6:11,12*

June 25
Devotion without self-discipline can contribute to emotionalism, irrational thinking, and impulsive behaviors. Balance devotional ardor with intellectual inquiry and commonsense behaviors.

June 26
Without awareness of our spiritual nature, attempts to regulate mental and emotional states and behaviors will be only partially successful. Know that you are superior to your thoughts, moods, and actions.

June 27
It can be helpful to consecrate a private place to be used only for prayer, meditation, and quiet reflection. When you are there, contemplate your true nature and relationship with the Infinite.

June 28
Established in calmness elicited by meditation practice, wisely live as one of God's agents.

June 29
Wholesome living, an orderly lifestyle, and emergence of superconsciousness during meditation purify the mind and consciousness.

June 30
Meditate regularly to have transcendent realizations.

Holding the body, head, and neck erect, motionless, steady, gazing into the spiritual eye; serene, fearless, established in self-control, with mental impulses quieted, concentrating on the Supreme Reality, the devotee should sit, devoted to the highest realization.
– *Bhagavad Gita 6:13,14*

A Self-Examination

Optimistic	[ ] Always	[ ] Usually	[ ] Seldom
Think Rationally	[ ] Always	[ ] Usually	[ ] Seldom
Emotionally Stable	[ ] Always	[} Usually	[ ] Seldom
Happy and Cheerful	[ ] Always	[ ] Usually	[ ] Seldom
Self-Confident	[ ] Always	[ ] Usually	[ ] Seldom
Constructive Actions and Behaviors	[ ] Always	[ ] Usually	[ ] Seldom
Wisely Decisive	[ ] Always	[ ] Usually	[ ] Seldom
Impulses Controlled	[ ] Always	[ ] Usually	[ ] Seldom
Awareness is Clear	[ ] Always	[ ] Usually	[ ] Seldom
Purposes are Easily Accomplished	[ ] Always	[ ] Usually	[ ] Seldom
Holistic* Living	[ ] Always	[ ] Usually	[ ] Seldom
Ideal Body Weight	[ ] Always	[ ] Usually	[ ] Seldom
Choose Nutritious Foods	[ ] Always	[ ] Usually	[ ] Seldom
Exercise Regularly	[ ] Always	[ ] Usually	[ ] Seldom
Wise Management of Money and All Material Things	[ ] Always	[ ] Usually	[ ] Seldom
Have Harmonious Relationships	[ ] Always	[ ] Usually	[ ] Seldom
Respect the Divine Nature of Others	[ ] Always	[ ] Usually	[ ] Seldom
Nurture the Environment	[ ] Always	[ ] Usually	[ ] Seldom
Profoundly Study Higher Realities	[ ] Always	[ ] Usually	[ ] Seldom
Meditate Daily	[ ] Always	[ ] Usually	[ ] Seldom

Endeavor to change "usually" and "seldom" to *always*.

*Emphasis on the whole and the interdependence of its parts.

Ellen Grace O'Brian and Roy Eugene Davis
installing portraits of Kriya Yoga gurus
at Center for Spiritual Enlightenment,
San Jose, California. *March 5, 2013*

JULY

July 1

Pray with devotion to become aware of God within and around you, then be still. Meditate in that realization of wholeness. After meditating, if you pray for guidance to have needs met or to accomplish purposes, pray for the welfare of others before you pray for yourself.

July 2

When praying for others, wish for their highest good rather than for specific results. Don't be inclined to use will power to cause effects or think that you know what is best for someone else. Avoid wanting to mentally control others. Wish for their spiritual awakening and fulfillment. Have faith that your prayers are influential.

July 3

Listen to Om. Meditate in Om. Absorb your attention in Om, then transcend it.

Affirm With Intention
I listen to Om, meditate in Om, absorb
my attention in Om, and transcend it.

There is a fundamental purpose for our lives.
To recognize it we must know where life comes
from and where it is going. We must look beyond
our immediate goals to what we ultimately want
to accomplish and consider life's highest
potential for development.
– *Paramahansa Yogananda*

July 4
When you pray, desire to have guidance. It will emerge from within you as inspired ideas, be revealed by words or actions of others, or be provided by events and opportunities that emerge. Discern the difference between inspired ideas and wishful thinking.

July 5
When praying to have needs met or to accomplish meaningful purposes, clearly define your needs and purposes in writing and keep a record of the results of prayer. This will focus your thoughts and actions and improve your confidence.

July 6
God is the only Reality. God's pure essence is individualized as souls. God's life enlivens the universe and living things. God's power expresses as energies, forces, and all manifestations of nature. There are no beings or powers apart from God.

July 7
Just as universes are produced from the expressive field of ultimate Reality, so our personal circumstances may be produced or attracted by our states of consciousness and mental states.

One should choose as a livelihood those activities which are consistent with *dharma* [that which upholds nature and society], adhere to the path of peace, and engage in studies to acquire useful knowledge. This is the way to happiness.
– *Charaka Samhita / Ancient Ayurvedic Text*

July 8

Flows of God's grace are inhibited when we are small-minded, irresponsible, or intellectually and physically lazy. Grace can flow freely when we are alertly Self-aware, mentally expansive, responsible for our thoughts and actions, intellectually discerning, and engaged in constructive actions. Complete trust in God makes us receptive to actions of grace.

July 9

Unwavering aspiration to be God-realized awakens dormant soul forces, clarifies the mind and awareness, and enables us to apprehend and experience the reality of God. When aspiration to be God-realized prevails, it is easier to make wholesome lifestyle choices.

July 10

Master thoughts by cultivating optimism and choosing to think constructively and rationally. Meditate to calm the mind and encourage its actions to be more orderly. Associate with healthy-minded people. Identify with and emulate the behaviors of role models who are spiritually aware and functionally competent.

July 11

Master states of consciousness by training yourself to go to sleep at will, awaken from sleep at a predetermined time, and immediately experience superconsciousness when you sit to meditate. Be Self-aware in the midst of activities. Avoid excessive identification with thoughts, moods, and circumstances.

Affirm With Decisive Intention
I am always aware of my true nature.

July 12
Cultivate even-mindedness and emotional stability in all situations. Don't allow memories of past misfortune or present perceptions of discord to disturb your inner peace. Avoid obsessive thinking, sad moods, or thoughts or feelings of despair. Live with meaningful purpose. Be happy. Be thankful for the opportunities you presently have to learn, creatively express, and actualize your spiritual potential.

July 13
Be thankful that you are free to choose your thoughts, feelings, and actions. Choose wisely.

July 14
The most effective approach to total wellness is a life-management program with thoughtful attention focused on spiritual, psychological, and physical health rather than to concentrate on one aspect and neglect all others. Be established in spiritual awareness.

July 15
Never affirm ill health, poverty, limitations of any kind, or inability to be freely functional. Remember that God is equally present everywhere and in and as all souls.

Declare With Realization
I acknowledge God's omnipresence
and affirm my radiant health, total
well-being, and freedom of expression.

From all blindness of heart, from pride, vainglory, and hypocrisy; from envy, hatred, and malice, and from all uncharitableness, Good Lord, deliver us.
– *The Book of Common Prayer / The Litany*

July 16
While we choose to identify with the limitations of the self-conscious state of awareness, they will tend to exist. What we presume to be true is what we are inclined to perceive and experience. Discard all considerations of limitation and express your divine nature. You can do it!

July 17
If we affirm that we are victims of our karma, inherited tendencies, planetary influences, or any other external cause, we are inclined to experience the results of our misunderstanding. Choose to be spiritually conscious and let your innate knowledge of invincibility prevail.

July 18
So long as we think and act like truth-seekers instead of truth-knowers we will be inclined to wander aimlessly through space and time. That which we seek is within, at the innermost level of our being.

July 19
Religious rituals and spiritual practices performed without understanding and conscious intention cannot produce satisfying results. Know why you do what you do and skillfully act to have the results you want to have.

Affirm With Firm Resolve
Renouncing all unrealistic notions and
impractical actions, I think rationally
and act wisely.

I never allow the word "impossible" to become
rooted in my mind; nor should you.
– *Paramahansa Yogananda*

July 20
The final knowledge that liberates us is Self-revealed in our illumined consciousness.

July 21
There are seven discernible stages through which souls awaken from ignorance of the truth about themselves to illumination of consciousness. To make spiritual growth easier, renounce behaviors and circumstances which restrict it, while cultivating behaviors and choosing circumstances which nurture it.

July 22
Unconsciousness is characteristic of the first stage of the soul's identification with matter, during which one is so completely identified with the mind and physical body that one mistakenly presumes to be a mind-body being. Some symptoms of this condition are mental dullness, apathy, boredom, and provincialism. Rigid beliefs and unreasoned opinions tend to prevail. Spiritual awareness is minimal. Intellectual powers are weak and undeveloped. If one is religious, prayer may be directed to one's mental concept of God. Blind belief in God and unrealistic salvation theories may be considered to be more important than knowledge. Spiritual fulfillment may be thought of as a far-distant future possibility. Activities are primarily survival-oriented or impelled by desires, whims, and peer-group influences. Memories, habits, learned or acquired behaviors, and social and cultural traditions tend to determine lifestyle. Life forces are mostly dormant.

July 23

Dysfunctional self-consciousness is characteristic of the second stage of soul awakening. Mental confusion along with irrational thinking and conflicted emotional states is common. Egocentric preoccupation with the mistaken sense of self-identity prevails. One may be superstitious, fascinated with magic, endeavor to acquire supernatural powers, believe in angels, or interested in mediumship or "channeling" in misguided endeavors to communicate with beings in other spheres who are supposed to have exceptional knowledge. Powers of intellectual discrimination are weak. Addictions, sensual desires, cravings, obsessions, hallucinations, emotionally dependent relationships, self-defeating thinking and behaviors, neurotic needs, complaints, fault-finding, and fantasies are common. Emotions and subconscious influences tend to determine thinking and behaviors. When meditating, one may be more interested in mental phenomena or having an emotional experience than spiritual growth. Life forces are only partially aroused.

Affirm With Determination
I am firmly resolved to quickly awaken through
all of the stages of spiritual growth to complete
liberation of consciousness.

At fifteen, my mind was inclined toward learning;
at thirty I stood firm; at forty, I was free from
delusions; at fifty, I understood the will of God;
at sixty, my ears were receptive to truth; at
seventy, I could follow the promptings of my heart
without overstepping the boundaries of right.
– *Confucius (551 – 478 B.C.E.)*

July 24
Functional self-consciousness is characteristic of the third stage of soul awakening: a more superior, healthy-minded, yet still egocentric condition. Rational, nurturing choices usually determine behaviors and relationships. Partial intellectual comprehension of the reality of God may be present, mixed with traditional beliefs and personal opinions. One may be more interested in accessing divine influences to acquire powers, improve functional skills, or control personal circumstances than Self-discovery and God-realization. Meditative contemplation and prayer may be directed to physical and psychological improvement only, or used to enhance abilities for the purpose of accomplishing personal goals. While one may be curious about the metaphysical causes of mundane events, and spiritual growth may be desired, interest in this-world projects and relationships tends to be more compelling. Some characteristics common to the first two stages of soul awakening may be influential. Soul forces are somewhat aroused and Self-knowledge may gradually emerge.

Affirm With Confidence
I easily see though all illusions and rise above
all modified states of mind and consciousness.

To be God-realized is to know your Self as the great
ocean of Spirit by dissolving the delusion that you
you are this little ego, body, and personality.
– *Paramahansa Yogananda*

July 25

Superconsciousness is characteristic of the fourth level of soul awakening. Superconscious states emerge during meditative contemplation and can be influential after meditation practice. False ideas of self-identity diminish as Self-knowing increases. Activities and relationships are wisely chosen and experienced without compulsion or attachments. Willingness to live righteously and to engage in spiritual practices is apparent. Solitude is enjoyable. Releasing mental and emotional attachments is easier. Sensory and mental impulses are more easily regulated. Unwholesome thoughts, conversations, and lifestyle habits; unethical behaviors; and the company of ego-directed people are no longer appealing. Aspiration to liberation of consciousness is sincere and constant. At this stage, one can be a competent disciple (learner) on the spiritual path. Some remaining characteristics common to the first three stages of soul awakening may interfere with endeavors to experience spiritual growth. These can be overcome by will power and choice, or transcended as soul qualities become more expressive. The soul's more fully aroused life forces flow upward through the spinal pathway into the higher brain centers.

The mistaken sense of self-identity disappears
when the difference between modified states of
consciousness, the influences of the attributes
of nature, and one's pure-conscious essence of
being is discerned. Awareness then flows
serenely to absolute freedom.
– *Patanjali's Yoga-Sutra 4:25,26*

July 26

Cosmic conscious perceptions are characteristic of the fifth level of soul awakening. As superconsciousness is more influential, egocentric inclinations are weakened. Meditative perceptions and realizations are inclined to be transcendent. The universe is known to be produced and maintained by emanated influences of primordial nature: Om with space, time, and fine cosmic particles. Activities and relationships are enjoyed with higher understanding. Enlarged soul capacities allow comprehension of higher realities. Soul abilities become more pronounced and are wisely used. Compassion for others and all forms of life is pronounced. The body's life forces flow easily, removing restrictions to spiritual growth from the mind and transforming the body to enable it to accommodate transcendent perceptions.

Declare With Appreciation

My improved intellectual powers and enhanced intuitive abilities increasingly enable me to directly know God's omnipotence, omnipresence, and omniscience.

There are some souls who cannot dwell upon nor engage their minds with any [transcendent] mystery; they are drawn to a certain gentle simplicity before God, and held in this simplicity, without other consideration save to know they are before God.

– *St. Francis of Sales (1567 – 1622)*

July 27
God-realization is characteristic of the sixth stage of soul awakening. Troublesome subconscious influences are easily resisted, weakened, and neutralized. Selfless, insightful actions prevent the accumulation of further troublesome mental impressions (karmic influences). Meditation is blissful and spontaneous as determined by one's inclination to be fully conscious and the impulses of grace. As God-realization increases, quick awakening to the final stage of spiritual enlightenment occurs.

July 28
The ultimate degree of soul awakening is permanent spiritual enlightenment that culminates in liberation of consciousness. Actions are spontaneously appropriate. Self-realization is not diminished by the purified ego-sense which remains as a viewpoint from which to dispassionately observe objective and subjective conditions while maintaining awareness of higher realities.

July 29
Spiritual growth is rapid when we wisely apply valid knowledge acquired from reliable sources and our Self-revealed knowledge.

Affirm With Conviction
I am completely committed to being fully Self- and God-realized in my current incarnation.

Focus your attention within. You will experience new power, new strength, and new peace in body, mind, and spirit. When you do this, all bonds that limit you will vanish.
– *Paramahansa Yogananda*

July 30
Our Self- and God-realization is not only for us. When we are fully spiritually enlightened, the processes of nature and all souls in all realms and dimensions of space and time will be beneficially influenced. To be of the greatest value to others and the environment, faithfully nurture your spiritual growth.

July 31
Time need not be a determining factor in relationship to spiritual growth. Many souls who have sojourned in the universe for thousands of years are still not conscious of their spiritual potential. Some are slowly, progressively awakening. You can quickly awaken if you really want to do so.

Emphatically Declare
I am rapidly awakening through the
stages of spiritual growth!

The only surer ground is direct experience
of God, which many persons claim to have.
Arguments lead to the base of the mountain,
experience alone scales it. He who has climbed
the peak gets an evidence—and a thrill
of summit-vision which the dwellers in
the valley ... can never have.
– *Rufus Jones (1863 – 1948)*
Religious Foundations

Lord, make me an instrument of Your peace.
Where there is hatred, let me sow love;
where there is injury, pardon;
where there is doubt, faith;
where there is despair, hope;
where there is darkness, light;
and where there is sadness, joy.
O divine Master, grant that I may not so
much seek to be consoled, as to console;
to be understood, as to understand;
to be loved, as to love.
For it is in giving that we receive;
it is in pardoning that we are pardoned;
and it is in dying that we are born to eternal life.*

Anonymous. First published in an obscure French spiritual magazine, *La Clochette*, in 1912 and later attributed to Saint Francis of Assisi (1181 – 1226).

* The dying (cessation) of a mistaken sense of self-identity allows our immortal essence of being (existence) to be realized.

BRONZE BODHISATTVA ICON
Sanskrit *bodhi*: “to know”; to be spiritually awake.
Sattva: pure, luminous.
Icon: symbolic representation of something.

AUGUST

August 1
Knowledge of higher realities innate to consciousness is the only reliable teacher. Others can only provide information. Our own Self-revealed knowledge liberates us.

August 2
Be rationally and intuitively decisive, confident, intentional, and skillfully effective in mastering your states of consciousness and behaviors. You can be superior to your mind, senses, and environmental influences.

August 3
Enlightened people can help us to be spiritually awake. Their behaviors can demonstrate how we can live. When we are intuitively receptive, some of their realizations may be wordlessly transmitted to us.

August 4
A guru's primary function is to help souls discard the erroneous notion of being other than a flawless, individualized unit of the pure essence of ultimate Reality.

I care not what terms you may use, be it Kindly Light, Providence, the Over-Soul, Omnipotence ... so long as we are agreed in regard to the great central fact itself, God then fills the universe ... and there is nothing that is outside.
– *William James (1842 – 1910)*

August 5
Guidelines for ethical living and spiritual practices that can reveal our innate qualities and Self-knowledge are for everyone, everywhere.

August 6
Emotionally immature truth seekers may be inclined to want to demonstrate their deluded individualism by fulfilling self-centered desires, expressing shallow personal opinions, and dramatizing their unrealistic sense of self-importance. Authentic spiritual growth purifies the ego, banishes false ideas, and impels us to always be higher purpose-directed. Awaken from the limitations of self-centered thinking. Quickly grow to emotional maturity.

August 7
Unlike invalid theories and passing fads that emerge, are popular for a brief duration of time and fade into obscurity, the laws of consciousness are timeless. God remains the same; souls are individualized units of the pure essence of ultimate Reality; insufficient spiritual awareness is the primary cause of human distress. Only authentic spiritual growth that culminates in Self-knowledge and God-realization can confer unwavering peace of mind and the permanent removal of delusions and illusions that cause suffering and misfortune.

August 8
Disciples (students, learners) on a spiritual path who renounce arrogance and allow egocentricity to diminish so that soul qualities can effortlessly emerge, experience rapid progress. Disciples who are not yet committed to actualizing authentic spiritual growth are inclined to be inattentive and attached to erroneous beliefs, personal opinions, and existing circumstances.

August 9
How is a guru to be found? If one is destined to have a personal relationship with such a spiritual teacher, it will happen. Until it does, it is best to prepare for it by virtuous living and concentrated spiritual practice while trusting the Source for guidance and support.

August 10
Some souls prefer limitation to freedom because they have doubts about their ability to have improved conditions. Ordinary (modified, blurred) states of awareness may allow us to feel insecure and inadequate. When we are Self-aware, it is easy to be confident, imagine ideal possibilities, and use our knowledge and skills.

August 11
If you are not yet enlightened, what will your life be like when you are fully awake to the truth of yourself and ultimate Reality? How will you think? What will you do? Think and act now like an enlightened person.

August 12
If God could speak in words, we might hear: "I am the unchanging Reality of all that is; I am the universe; I am all beings; I am you. Though I express in diverse ways, I am undivided, am not in the least influenced by events occurring in my Self-manifested realms, and am forever the impartial witness of all that occurs."

If you see things in eternity, you are less a prey
to the pain of their passing, so you can learn the
more easily not to clutch at them as they pass.
– *Gerald Vann (1906 – 1963)*

August 13
God "speaks" to us—not in the language of the mind but in the language of our essence—as impulses arising from the core of our innermost being that incline us to Self-discovery and spiritual growth.

August 14
Our affirmative response to the opportunity we have to choose to be Self-realized arouses our spiritual forces, causes constructive adjustments of mental attitudes and states of consciousness, and empowers us to persist on the spiritual path with unwavering faith that our right endeavors will bring forth ideal results.

August 15
Even if aspiration to be Self-realized is weak, sincere desire to know the reality of God will cause supportive events to unfold to fulfill that desire.

August 16
If you are unable to immediately discern the truth about yourself in relationship to the Infinite, meditatively contemplate your true nature and ultimate Reality until your understanding improves.

August 17
That which endures without changing is said to be real. Expecting transient things, situations, or relationships to provide lasting security or happiness will always result in discomfort or disappointment.

Great Truths are portions of the soul … ;
Great souls are portions of Eternity.
– *James Russell Lowell (1819 – 1891)*

August 18
If thoughts are irrational and emotions are unsettled, it is difficult to regulate mental and physical impulses. On such occasions, it can be helpful to pray and meditate to infuse the transformational influences of awakened soul awareness into the mind.

August 19
The “ancestor” of desires is egocentricity. When that is not nurtured with attention, it diminishes. When soul qualities are nurtured by constant Self-remembrance, only constructive, life-enhancing thoughts and inclinations arise in the mind.

August 20
God-surrendered devotees don’t waste energy or time in idle daydreaming, purposeless talk, or any other kind of useless actions. Their attention and actions are directed to practices that result in psychological transformation and spiritual growth.

August 21
When we know that we can choose and immediately assume any state of consciousness at will, we are free from self-defeating beliefs that there are causes external to ourselves that can determine or affect our lives.

August 22
Obsessive concern about unimportant matters and dramatization of addictive mental attitudes and behaviors are symptoms of egocentric willfulness and emotional immaturity. Be responsible for what you think and do.

Affirm With Confidence
I completely renounce all debilitating mental attitudes, beliefs, opinions, behaviors, and activities.

August 23
Every soul will be fully restored to omnipresence and omniscience. Only Ultimate Reality is omnipotent.

August 24
An unenlightened spiritual aspirant's primary obstacle to overcome is tenacious attachment to the erroneous idea that one is other than a flawless unity of the pure essence of ultimate Reality. When this primary error of the intellect is corrected, the products of ignorance of the truth cease to exist.

August 25
The most efficient way to change unwanted or troublesome mental states and psychological conditions is to determine their causes and remove them. If this cannot easily be done, focused endeavors that will improve mental and emotional states and personal behaviors can and should be implemented.

August 26
To overcome self-centeredness and be relieved of difficulties related to it, expand your awareness. Choose worthwhile endeavors for which to use your knowledge, skills, energies, and resources. Be fully committed to spiritual growth. Invite God to work through you.

August 27
If resolve for spiritual growth is weak, the mind's self-serving tendencies are inclined to become stronger and more influential. When resolve for spiritual growth is strong and firm, superconscious influences prevail over conflicted psychological states.

August 28
Self-revealed knowledge makes the soul impervious to the effects of mundane causes and spiritual growth is steadily progressive.

August 29
Even a little attention and endeavor directed to right living and spiritual practice results in spiritual growth that soon puts us into a relationship with the currents of evolution and the impulses of God's grace.

August 30
The spiritual aspirant who is not inspired may practice meditation as a rehearsed ritual that is seldom productive of worthwhile results. To ensure highest benefits, meditate with inspired intention. Desire nothing but to be Self- and God-realized.

August 31
Until the mind is completely illumined, emotions and urges nourished by memories of prior experiences may influence the mind to elicit nonuseful desires, fantasies, and hallucinations. These can be resisted, restrained, weakened, and removed by disciplined living and by refined superconscious states which become pronounced when we meditate regularly.

Affirm With Realization
God is my life and I know it.
My purpose in this world is to awaken in God
and I am resolved to do it. Forsaking all things
which are unimportant, I direct my attention
and dedicate myself to God-realization.

GANESHA
Remover of obstacles; lord of wisdom
and ruler of new beginnings.
Sanskrit *gana*, multitude, and *isha*, lord or ruler.
Created by artisans in Jaipur, India.
Solid white marble, two feet high.

SEPTEMBER

September 1
When subliminal impulses that stimulate the mind and emotions and interfere with concentration are weakened and become still, our pure essence of being can be Self-shining. This realization can spontaneously occur at any time and be nurtured by attentive meditation.

September 2
Forceful endeavors to suppress disturbing thoughts and moods are futile. The effective way to regulate thoughts and emotional states is to act decisively in the course of everyday living and daily superconsciously meditate.

September 3
A Self-realized person is always calmly poised and able to observe events with dispassionate objectivity.

September 4
When we are calmly peaceful, the transformative effects of superconscious meditation can continue to refine our nervous system, purify our mind, and illumine our consciousness while we attend to our duties.

Affirm With Realization
The radiant purity of my essence of being continuously illumines my mind and consciousness.

In the highest consciousness, you can maintain your divine realizations while working, speaking, or moving about in this world. When that is accomplished, there is no possibility of falling back into delusion.
– *Paramahansa Yogananda*

September 5
The trends of evolution are driven by the power of the expressive aspect of ultimate Reality. When we are in harmony with trends of evolution, rapid spiritual growth and constant good fortune are more easily experienced.

September 6
Although our true nature is not directly affected by our actions or spiritual practices, its capacities expand and its qualities more quickly emerge when our effective actions remove or enable us to transcend physical and mental conditions which confine and restrict them.

September 7
Adjustments of mental states and states of consciousness are constructive actions originated at subtle and fine levels that can have useful physical effects. At the finest level of Self-awareness, your intentions alone can produce and attract the results you want to have.

September 8
Restlessness, erroneous ideas, emotional conflicts, and other conditions that may modify the surface of our awareness don't influence our pure, true nature, just as events that occur in the universe don't influence the pure essence of ultimate Reality.

Let your devotion to God be like a wood fire that burns steadily for a long time; not like a straw fire that produces a bright flame and quickly dies out.
– *Paramahansa Yogananda*

September 9
A spiritual path is most effective when it is compatible with our psychological temperament and our capacity to beneficially use the recommended practices.

September 10
A problem cannot be satisfactorily solved by the states of consciousness and actions which produced it. To solve problems—including the primary problem of lack of spiritual awareness—learn to see solutions and do what is necessary to have them actualized.

September 11
Some people desire a relationship with God because they need healing or improvement of personal circumstances. Some desire only material gain. Some want enough understanding to enable them to have a more satisfying human experience or to provide hope for an afterlife. The wisdom-impelled devotee ardently aspires to complete God-realization. Let wisdom light your way.

September 12
Cosmic perceptions emerge in our awareness when we meditate deeply. The pure essence of God is known as the essence of all souls; the all-pervading reality of God is apprehended as including all souls within itself.

Affirm With Conviction
At the deepest level of my essence of being
I am always pure, whole, and Self-knowing.

Only for God wait thou in stillness ....
– *The Book of Psalms 62:5*

September 13
Perceptions and experiences during and after transition from the body will be determined by our degree of Self-realization and our mental and emotional states. If our awareness is not clear and peaceful during transition, subtle mental impulses may cause confusion. It will be best to calmly meditate, surrendered to the process with aspiration to awaken to pure consciousness.

September 14
The light of consciousness that shines within us can be merged with our awareness when leaving the body. Daily superconscious meditation is the best preparation for eventual departure from this realm.

September 15
Think and speak about what you want to experience; don't think or talk about unwanted experiences. Avoid gossip. Acknowledge your innate divinity and look for it in others. Don't complain about your problems or about unwanted circumstances. Enlarge your consciousness. Use your imagination and skills to be problem-free and always have ideal circumstances.

September 16
When we pray, believing God to be a being distinct from us, some desires can be fulfilled according to our belief. It is then not God who fulfills desire, but ourselves—by assuming a point of view which enables us to perceive and acknowledge desired outcomes. Without belief and acceptance of the results for which we pray, our prayers are powerless to be transformative. Believe that desired results are possible and you can have them.

September 17
Be respectful and courteous toward others while avoiding excessive or unnecessary social activities. Behind the personality characteristics, words, and behaviors of every person is the pure light of their essence of being.

September 18
Remember that the primary purpose of your life in this world is to awaken to God-realization. What are you doing to be spiritually enlightened?

September 19
The River of Time is swallowing your material life and preparing you for your ultimate freedom in God. Live wisely, remembering your spiritual destiny.

September 20
Awareness of wholeness with thoughts of God purifies the mind and results in conscious attunement with the Infinite.

September 21
Our divine qualities can be actualized by remembering our relationship with the Infinite and living so that we are always in tune with the rhythms of life.

Affirm With Conviction
I am supported by the rhythms of life.

The laws of life can teach us to live peacefully with Nature and with our innate characteristics. When we know the laws, and conduct ourselves accordingly, we can live in lasting happiness, good health, and harmony with all life and with ourselves.
– *Paramahansa Yogananda*

September 22
Clear awareness of the reality of God can be constant. The ultimate extent of emergence of innate knowledge enables us to completely comprehend the truth about God and the processes of life.

September 23
Constructive desires, which, when fulfilled, enhance our lives and clarify our awareness, are not detrimental to our spiritual growth. Desires impelled by ignorance and insatiable cravings are definitely harmful. Have only constructive desires.

September 24
As a hungry person needs food, as a thirsty person needs water, as a person who is deprived of air needs air, so with that urgency should be our need to know and experience God.

September 25
When our love for someone is constant, we think of them often. When our love for God is like that, thoughts of God are always present. Loving thoughts of God keep us attuned with God.

September 26
All souls are individualized units of God's being and all minds are units of God's Cosmic Mind. You are always in God and have a relationship with God's Mind.

While you are learning to swim in the sea of life,
you can help others learn to swim.
– *Paramahansa Yogananda*

September 27
Until Self-realization is permanent, frequently remind yourself that you exist in God.

September 28
To always have a supportive relationship with cosmic mind, think clearly and constructively. Notice when it is responsive to your thoughts, intentions, desires, and needs. You will then learn to understand the subjective causes of your daily experiences and circumstances.

September 29
If your goals and projects are clearly defined and you want them to manifest, expect cosmic mind to respond and it will. If you cannot clearly define what you want or need, expect cosmic mind to produce circumstances for your highest good and it will. You have a divine right to be healthy, happy, successful, and spiritually awake.

September 30
Believe that you will experience rapid spiritual growth. Contemplate ultimate Reality and your pure essence of being until realization blossoms.

Affirm With Realization
I am always healthy, happy, successful,
and spiritually awake!

The consciousness of God's presence
is the first principle of religion.
– *Hebrew Proverb*

PARAMAHANSA YOGANANDA
Late 1940s

OCTOBER

October 1
The spiritual basis of real prosperity is to know that the universe is an undivided manifestation of cosmic forces emanating from and sustained by an ultimate Reality.

October 2
Prosperity is constant when we are fully conscious of the wholeness of life, our desires are easily fulfilled, and our needs are easily provided for by our skillful endeavors and freely expressive impulses of grace.

October 3
If you are reluctant to be prosperous, examine your thoughts and feelings to discover why you are denying yourself opportunities to live freely. Replace poverty thoughts and feelings with prosperity ideas and feelings reinforced with intentional, productive actions.

October 4
To be prosperous is to experience total well-being: to have what we need for physical comfort; be mentally, emotionally, and physically healthy; free from addictive tendencies and behaviors; and able to live effectively with meaningful purpose.

October 5
When you think about the near and distant future, do you think about ideal circumstances and freedom of expression, or do you imagine unsatisfactory conditions and inability to accomplish purposes? Be a possibility-thinker. Imagine your highest good and actualize it.

October 6

Nurture your soul qualities. Enlarge your capacity to easily accept health, happiness, and accomplishment as being natural for you to experience. Nothing external to you can prevent you from being fulfilled.

October 7

With knowledge that subtle elements and cosmic forces compose material things, learn to easily relate to the world. Be responsible for your choices and actions. Wisely use resources that are available to you.

October 8

When planning endeavors, imagine desired outcomes as they will be when they are accomplished. Perform actions that will produce or attract desired results. What can be vividly imagined, believed as possible, and accepted in fact, can be actualized. Plan without limitations.

Affirm With Thankfulness

The higher knowledge, prosperity, and freedom that I have, I sincerely wish for everyone, everywhere.

I salute the supreme teacher, the Truth, whose nature is bliss; who is the giver of the highest happiness; who is pure wisdom; beyond all qualities and infinite; beyond words; one and eternal; pure and still; beyond all change and phenomena; the silent witness to our thoughts and emotions. I salute Truth, the supreme teacher.

– *Ancient Vedic Hymn*

October 9
Efficiently manage your activities, energy, relationships, and money so that your life is always well-ordered and productive.

October 10
Keep your mind and awareness pure by nurturing kind thoughts and feelings for others, compassion for their misfortune, and happiness for their well-being. Be emotionally calm and mentally peaceful at all times.

October 11
When confused, afraid, anxious, emotionally upset, or overwhelmed by circumstances, turn within. Be still. Meditate in the deep silence until you are calm and can view circumstances objectively. Rest to restore your reserves of energy. Pray for inner strength, insight, guidance, and spiritual renewal.

October 12
Most human problems and limitations are due to lack of spiritual awareness. Improve your awareness and knowledge of your real Self and ultimate Reality. Remind yourself that you are in this world to be spiritually awake and express your knowledge and abilities.

October 13
The states of consciousness and mental and emotional states you choose determine your circumstances, relationships, and actions. What are you choosing now?

Affirm With Intention
I choose to be spiritually awake, mentally alert,
and emotionally calm.

October 14
Aware of your true nature, acknowledge that you *have* what you need for your well-being and fulfillment. Self-contentment, rational thinking, and emotional maturity provide a firm foundation for effective living and progressive spiritual growth.

October 15
When you need healing of any kind, remember that your consciousness of wholeness can include your mind, body, and circumstances. Don't allow mistaken beliefs about karma or other false ideas to limit you.

October 16
Your mental concepts of what you are will change as you have insights into your true nature and relationship with the Infinite. Realizations can prevail over illusional perceptions and false ideas.

October 17
Redeem your awareness from memories of hardship, traumatic events, failures, and misfortune. Restore it to wholeness by viewing memories with objectivity and nurturing Self-knowledge. Don't allow any past events to adversely influence your thoughts or behaviors today.

Affirm With Confidence
Always firmly established in Self-awareness,
I think constructively, act responsibly, have
constant good fortune, and experience
progressive spiritual growth.

All that is, is God. The different forms of
existence are God's myriad manifestations.
– *Kabir (1440 –1518)*

October 18
When unpleasant memories cause you distress, rest in soul awareness and view them with detachment. If you cannot immediately do this, breathe deeply a few times until you are peacefully comfortable. Remember your innate divine nature. Anchor your awareness in God.

October 19
Just as objects in front of a light cause shadows of the objects to appear, so our mental images may project the shadows of our circumstances on the screen of space-time. Because thoughts and beliefs are more real than their effects, unwanted circumstances can be changed by adjusting our mental states.

October 20
To change or improve external conditions, imagine them as you want them to be, feel (be aware and have conviction) that you have them, and perform helpful actions when necessary to do so.

October 21
If circumstances and relationships aren't satisfactory, why are you allowing them in your life? Imagine what you want or need and produce or attract it.

Affirm With Decisive Resolve
I am responsible for my thoughts, feelings,
behaviors, experiences, and circumstances.

I am not the guru. God is the guru,
I am God's servant.
– *Paramahansa Yogananda*

October 22
If we are unable to live effectively, it is unlikely that we will be able to experience satisfying spiritual growth. A success-attitude, constructive behaviors, and powers of concentration that enable us to proficiently accomplish worthwhile mundane purposes can also enable us to have rapid spiritual growth.

October 23
If you can admit that you do not know, you are already wiser than those who believe that they have knowledge they do not yet possess.

October 24
If we are not prospering—if we are not as healthy, happy, successful, and prosperous as we would like to be—it may be that we actually know better than we do; that we have to appropriately use the knowledge and skills we already have.

October 25
By performing actions skillfully you can have enhanced powers of concentration, improved functional abilities, and be creatively responsive to all situations. Being able to function effectively is one of the positive side-benefits of authentic spiritual growth.

October 26
Wisely choose your friends and associates. Honor the innate divine nature of everyone while nurturing only the intimate personal relationships that are for your highest good and the highest good of others. You have ideals to actualize and a spiritual destiny to fulfill. Provide the most constructive circumstances that will enable you to accomplish your worthy purposes.

October 27
Even in the midst of relationships and activities, you are always alone with the Infinite. No one else can think your thoughts, dream your noble dreams, or experience your spiritual awakening and enlightenment.

October 28
Always do your best, then let God do the rest. You can do much to help yourself be fulfilled. If you do it, grace can and will do what you cannot do.

October 29
Life can provides us with what we ask for and are able to accommodate. If prosperity seems to be avoiding you, perhaps you have not yet asked for it, or perhaps you have asked but have not prepared yourself to have it. Fearlessly ask life for that which you deserve. Expand your capacity to accept and have.

October 30
Remove all obstacles to fulfillment and you will surely be fulfilled. Obstacles which are too resistant for you to remove, let God remove.

Affirm With Intention
I am always receptive to having and experiencing what is for my highest good.

Standing on the bare ground … my head bathed by the blithe air, and uplifted in the infinite space … all mean egotism vanishes … I am nothing; I see all; the currents of the Universal Being circulate through me. I am part and parcel of God.
– Ralph Waldo Emerson (1803 – 1882)

October 31

Whether we give to others the gift of our good will, our soulful prayers, constructive advice and encouragement, practical assistance, financial support, or other material things, giving should always be thoughtful, appropriate, and of value to the recipient of our compassionate acts without any thought or desire for personal recognition or reward. The moment we appropriately give is our moment of blessing. It is then that we are in the flow of life's supportive processes. We should give generously from our awareness of wholeness, viewing ourselves as but agents of ultimate Reality which freely provides.

Affirm With Conviction

The radiant purity of my essence of being
is freely expressive in and through me.
It illumines my mind and consciousness,
vitalizes my body, inspires my creative
ideas, empowers my constructive actions,
and enables me to gracefully grow to
emotional and spiritual maturity.

A human body has the highest evolutionary value
because of unique brain and spinal centers which
enable a person to fully grasp and express the
highest aspects of divinity.

– *Swami Sri Yukteswar*

SRI YANTRA

Sanskrit *sri*, “to shine.” Used to indicate respect or reverence for a person or thing.
Yantra, a geometrical pattern of circles, lotus petals, and triangles in a square to contain their energies.

Downward pointing triangles represent the emergence of cosmic powers into nature; upward pointing triangles represent the return of cosmic powers to their source.

Yantras may be drawn or painted on paper, canvas, or other materials, or engraved on metal. If the Yantra is visualized during meditative contemplation, it is to be eventually dissolved into one’s consciousness, as all material things are said to dissolve and disappear into That from which they came into manifestation.

Members and spiritual friends after a Kriya Yoga
initiation service at CSA headquarters

NOVEMBER

November 1
Some people believe their approach to God-realization to be the only way. Modes of worship and spiritual practice are outer forms often determined by cultural influences, opinions, preferences, and psychological temperament. The inner way is the emergence of Self-awareness.

November 2
At the core of all inspired religious and enlightenment traditions is the essence which empowers the teachings, arouses soul forces, and illumines consciousness.

November 3
We can never know the precise moment when we will awaken to God-realization. Be alert and watchful.

November 4
Arrested emotional growth is an obstacle to spiritual growth. Inability, or unwillingness, to be responsible for thoughts and behaviors may result in provincial mental attitudes and inclinations to want dependent relationships to satisfy immature emotional needs. Be willing to quickly grow to emotional maturity.

Affirm With Conviction
I am always alert and receptive to having
worthwhile insights and realizations that
enhance my life and allow me to more
quickly be spiritually enlightened.

November 5
Rigid mental attitudes and harmful habits confine soul awareness and may be transmitted to others and from one generation to another. Avoid them.

November 6
The cure for the "illness" of modified consciousness is Self-knowledge that blossoms into God-realization.

November 7
A primary cause of difficulties that some devotees have in their endeavors to comprehend spiritual realities and to express soul qualities is their attachment to ordinary, conditioned states of consciousness which contracts and blurs awareness and dulls the mind and intellect.

November 8
When our attention is preoccupied with externals, we may tend to forget our real nature and be excessively involved with superficial or unimportant relationships and circumstances. Learn to be soul-centered and have the freedom of unconfined awareness.

November 9
Our intellectual faculty, when pure, accurately reflects the luminosity of our essence of being.

November 10
When our faculties of perception are purified, we can acknowledge all that is true. When our perceptions are flawed because of inattentiveness or preconceived ideas, we tend to notice only those conditions which reinforce our delusions and illusions.

November 11
Train yourself to perceive with accuracy. Choose to see order, harmony, the inner causes of outer effects, and the many opportunities for learning and growth that life is always providing for you.

November 12
When you are soul-centered and happy, all people are benefited by your Self-knowledge and happiness. Let your soul light freely shine.

November 13
The most beneficial way to help others is to first help yourself to be God-realized. Go deeper in God.

November 14
Although soul awareness is outside of time, when we are still mind-body identified, time is a determining factor in our lives. Use the period of time that remains for you in this incarnation to awaken in eternity.

November 15
Our body, senses, mind, and intellect function because our consciousness pervades and enlivens them. We are superior to them just as ultimate Reality is superior to all through which it expresses.

November 16
When tempted to delay or to avoid your spiritual studies and practices, remind yourself of the importance of awakening to Self-knowledge. Arouse your inner forces and use will power. If you willingly and skillfully do what you know you must do to succeed, failure is an impossibility.

November 17
We need not compare our meditative perceptions or experiences with those claimed by others. Aspire only to be fully Self-realized.

November 18
Some obvious indications of spiritual growth are peace of mind, unwavering faith, emotional stability, courage, cheerful optimism, absence of addictive inclinations and behaviors, enhanced appreciation for life and living, and effective performance of constructive actions. Nurture these characteristics.

November 19
When we experience states of awareness which are more clear, we perceive ourselves differently in relationship to the world and to others. Values and goals may change. Time may be required to become used to new ways of perceiving, thinking, and relating. Learn by practice and experimentation how to adapt to the useful changes you experience. Be patient as you progress.

November 20
As your ego-awareness fades, you will be better able to accomplish Self-directed purposes. Perform constructive actions without attachment to them or their results.

November 21
Your essence is to be realized (experienced and known) rather than thought of as something you have. You don't have a soul or an essence; it is what you are.

Affirm With Realization
Yes! I am an immortal, spiritual being!

November 22
Fearlessness is characteristic of one who is devoted to the spiritual path. Believe in your Self. Believe in God. Know that, because God's grace has brought you to your present station in life, it will continue to provide for you.

November 23
Neither mind nor personality have independent power. God's power expressive in the universe is within you at the core of your being. Never say that you are powerless.

November 24
Materialists say that our sense of self-identity is a product of our brain and will no longer exist when our brain stops functioning. By superconscious realizations, experience your immortal essence which is other than a brain-mind-body illusion.

November 25
The all-pervading Reality of God is knowable and can be experienced. Mental restlessness obscures awareness of that Reality. Quiet the activities of the restless mind and God will be real to you.

November 26
Because God is expressing as souls, we can never be separated from God. Thoughts and/or feelings of being apart from God arise because of lack of accurate knowledge. When we experience God's presence, it may seem that we have been united with God. The truth is that we have always been in God.

November 27
Memories of meditative insights can remind us of what is possible to experience and inspire us to be more alert and intentional when we meditate. Be thankful for the insights you have had while looking forward to having more liberating perceptions and experiences.

November 28
People whose minds are strongly influenced by inertia are as though hypnotized. Inclined to think that having a continuing series of problems and limiting situations is normal, they are unable to imagine the freedom they could choose to have. Choose freedom.

November 29
From the very first moment when we became involved with the realm of mind and matter, we were destined to eventually awaken from unconscious identification with it and have our awareness restored to wholeness. Is now the moment in time for you to awaken?

Affirm With Confidence
I am rapidly awakening to realization
of my pure, serene, wholeness.

The eyes of my soul were opened, and I discerned
the fullness of God, in which I understood the
whole world, here and beyond the sea, brimming
over with wonder and cried out with a loud voice
"The whole world is full of God."
– *Angela of Foligno (1248 – 1309)*

November 30

When meditating, during the first stage of awakening to intuitively perceived knowledge, one can become aware of mental influences that need to be neutralized. At the second stage, troublesome mental influences have been weakened to the extent that they no longer interfere with endeavors to concentrate. The third stage is higher superconsciousness which makes possible examination of subtle and fine levels of consciousness. The fourth stage is Self-realization which enables the meditator to clearly comprehend the relationship of soul to mind and to internal and external phenomena. At the fifth stage, mental influences no longer cause changes in the mind or awareness. The sixth stage is God-realization. At the seventh stage one is firm in realization of pure being.

Affirm With Realization

As I superconsciously meditate, easily detaching
attention and awareness from objective conditions,
emotions, and thoughts, my consciousness is
quickly restored to its original, pure wholeness.

I call that mind free which escapes the bondage
of matter, which instead of stopping at the
material universe and making it a prison wall,
passes beyond to its Author...

– *William Ellery Channing (1780 – 1842)*

Everything in nature contains all the powers of nature.
– Ralph Waldo Emerson (1803 – 1882)

DECEMBER

December 1
Contemplation is calm "looking at" something with alert expectation of discovery. Meditatively contemplate what you want to know until insight emerges.

December 2
When we are not established in Self-awareness, we are inclined to be preoccupied with mental concepts, moods, and/or objective phenomena.

December 3
Be intentional when you sit to meditate. Have a specific way to start the practice session and immediately begin with firm resolve.

December 4
When you meditate, avoid preoccupation with thoughts and emotional states. Be disinterested in them, detach your attention from them, or be involved with a form of meditation practice (prayerful, affirmative, subtle sound contemplation, pranayama, or your preferred way) until your attention is completely focused or you experience thought-free superconsciousness.

December 5
Be firmly established in your spiritual practices by fervently aspiring to be fully, spiritually awake and doing things that allow spiritual growth to more easily occur.

Affirm With Conviction
I am alertly receptive to learning and discovery.

December 6
Clinging to an illusional sense of self-identity restricts spiritual awakening. Awareness can be quickly restored to wholeness by contemplating our pure essence of being until it is fully realized.

December 7
During meditation, learn to detach your attention from objective (outer) and subjective (mental) conditions and be conscious only of joyous, conscious existence.

December 8
After meditating, endeavor to remain aware of your pure essence of being.

December 9
When an effective meditation method is learned, it can be used repeatedly with benefit. Attentive practice of a meditation technique calms the mind and allows superconsciousness to be experienced.

December 10
Erroneous ideas may be acquired from others or be produced by irrational or "lazy" thinking. Discard all flawed ideas and use your powers of discriminative intelligence to know what is true.

December 11
When desire to be Self-realized prevails over all other inclinations and desires when you meditate, it will be easy to concentrate effectively.

Affirm With Determination
I am always inspired and highly Self-motivated
to live skillfully and meditate effectively.

December 12
Spiritual enlightenment is not our personal accomplishment. It is the result of the spontaneous Self-revelations that emerge when our mind and awareness are pure.

December 13
Self-realization is permanent when all troublesome subconscious influences are neutralized, erroneous ideas no longer arise in the mind, and perceptions are accurate.

December 14
Knowledge acquired by observation, reason, reflection, experimentation, or from others, may be flawed or misinterpreted. Knowledge of higher realities that emerges in our purified awareness is accurate.

December 15
Because there is a relationship between states of consciousness and physiological states, we can elicit superconsciousness by regulating physiological states during meditation practice. One easy way to do it is to observe the natural rhythms of breathing. When breathing is slow and subtle, notice the spaces between streams of thoughts, and "be there." Patient practice will enable you to assume a viewpoint of thought-free awareness at will. Productive meditation can then be effortless.

December 16
Frequent experiences of superconsciousness will quickly illumine your mind and awareness and unveil and bring forth your innate Self-knowledge.

Affirm With Realization
I easily rise above all modified states
of mind and consciousness.

December 17
Being aware of and feeling the higher chakras (dorsal, cervical, spiritual eye, and crown chakra) during meditation and at other times can help keep your awareness clear and be inspired and constructively motivated.

December 18
Meditation is undisturbed concentration that can result in identification of attention and awareness with what is contemplated or a transcendent realization without the support of an object of perception.

December 19
During the *final stages* of spiritual awakening, desire for liberation should be absent because desire that arises from egocentric awareness helps to sustain the flawed idea of independent existence.

December 20
Some souls are incarnated with the capacity to quickly awaken. Spiritual growth can be fast when we fervently aspire to be fully enlightened and are fully dedicated to right living and effective spiritual practice.

Affirmation
With spiritual enlightenment as my highest aim, I am fully dedicated to right living and effective spiritual practice.

I maintain that it is a common error among spiritual persons not to withdraw from outward things from time to time to worship God within themselves.
– *Brother Lawrence (1611 – 1691)*
The Practice of the Presence of God

December 21
Some people who have the capacity to quickly awaken to Self-knowledge neglect their opportunity or allow themselves to be distracted from it. Others, for whom circumstances were not so favorable, steadily progress because of their willingness to learn and unwavering dedication to their spiritual path.

December 22
Intellectual and intuitive insights improve our understanding of our true nature and our relationship with the Infinite, and enable us to think more rationally.

December 23
When we are enlightened, we know the truth about our essence of being and ultimate Reality. All enlightened souls have the same knowledge of higher realities.

December 24
States of consciousness are temporary conditions. Only complete awakening to pure consciousness can satisfy our aspiration to be completely free.

December 25
God's reality pervades the universe without being limited by it. When we are permanently God-conscious, we are not confined to this or any realm. While relating appropriately to this world, we can remain fully aware of our omnipresence.

Affirm With Realization
I enlarge my consciousness
to reclaim omnipresence.

Cast all your cares on God; that anchor holds.
– *Alfred, Lord Tennyson (1809 – 1892)*

December 26
What was your awareness of Self-identify before you forgot what you are? Behind the screen of your personality and mind, what is your real nature?

December 27
When we continue to believe that God is apart from us, we limit our capacity to know God as God is.

December 28
All of the actions of God's self-manifested universe are flawlessly ordered in accord with natural laws. Living in harmony with the rhythms of life results in total well-being and allows spiritual growth to occur naturally.

December 29
Nurturing devotion, seeking and acquiring knowledge of God, and performing spiritual practices and charitable acts, are helpful as means to awakening to Self- and God-realization.

December 30
How can we know when we are truly God-realized? The answer is self-evident: when we are, we know.

December 31
After quiet meditation, write list of worthwhile things to do and purposes to accomplish next year and far beyond. Do what you can to have them actualized while being receptive to unplanned good fortune that you will have.

Affirm With Quiet Enthusiasm
Established in Self- and God-awareness,
I go forward with inspired resolve and faith.

Notes

You could show me a beautiful nature scene
and I might be able to find some fault in it, but
I would prefer to look for that which is lovely
and harmonious.

– *Paramahansa Yogananda*

Notes

Don't allow your mind to be disturbed by what others do or say. Don't look back. Don't look to the right or to the left. Look straight ahead to the goal [of Self-realization], and go all the way in this incarnation. You can do it.

– Paramahansa Yogananda's final personal, spoken instruction to the author.
Early 1952, Twentynine Palms, California

Notes

Life is a perpetual Revelation
of the Infinite, Invisible One.
– *Bronson Alcott (1799 – 1888)*

Notes

The Eternal Gospel is the endless revelation
… of a spiritual Reality … over all and in all,
at the same time vastly more than things
in space and time … both immanent and
transcendent.

– *Rufus Jones (1863 – 1948)*
The Eternal Gospel

Notes

Every morning the day is reborn among the newly blossomed flowers with the same message retold and the same assurance renewed that death eternally dies, that the waves of turmoil are on the surface, and that the sea of tranquility is fathomless.

– *Rabindranath Tagore (1861 – 1941)*
Sadhana

Notes

The Masters say that the soul has two faces. The higher one always sees God, the lower one looks down and informs the senses. The higher one is the summit of the soul, it gazes into eternity.

– *Meister Eckhart (1260 – 1327)*

Notes

Let us respectfully contemplate the self-shining Reality of That which produces and nourishes the worlds and all life—and its pure essence of which we are expressive units.

Books by Roy Eugene Davis / CSA Press

Paramahansa Yogananda As I Knew Him
Seven Lessons in Conscious Living
The Eternal Way: The Inner Meaning
of the Bhagavad Gita
The Science of Self-Realization: Patanjali's Yoga-Sutra
Satisfying Our Innate Desire to Know God
English and Sanskrit Words and Philosophical
Concepts to Know

UNITED KINGDOM
Gazelle Book Services
sales@gazellebooks.co.uk
ITALY
Italian Language: www.marcovalerio.it
GERMANY
German language: www.kriya-yoga.de
INDIA
English Language Editions:
Motilal Banasidass www.mlbd.com
B. Jain Publishers www.bjainbooks.com
Indian Books Centre www.indianbookscentre.com
English and Hindi:
www.fullcirclebooks.in
TURKEY
Turkish Language:
Bilyay Vakfi www.bilyay.or.tr
English Language:
sabihabetul@bilincliyasam.org.tr
SPANISH LANGUAGE
Read and download free books at: www.csa-davis.org
Also articles in English, German, Italian,
Portuguese, French, Turkish, and Hindi

Center for Spiritual Awareness

Founded in 1972 by Roy Eugene Davis, world headquarters is located in the northeast Georgia mountains, 90 miles north of Atlanta. Facilities include offices and publishing department, the Shrine of All Faiths meditation temple, main meditation hall and dining room, library, learning resource center, bookstore, and six guest houses. Meditation retreats are scheduled from early spring until late autumn, on a donation basis.

For a free literature packet with a sample issue of *Truth Journal* magazine, information about Mr. Davis' books, DVDs, and CDS, and meditation seminar and retreat schedules contact:

Center for Spiritual Awareness
P. O. Box 7 Lakemont, Georgia 30552-0001
Phone 706-782-4723 weekdays 8 a.m. – 3 p.m.
e-mail: info@csa-davis.org
Or visit www.csa-davis.org
click on *Free Literature*

Shrine of All Faiths Meditation Temple

Center for Spiritual Awareness

Lakemont, Georgia